WRITING STYLES: GRADE 3
TABLE OF CONTENTS

P9-DEW-215

Peterborough Elementary School
17 High Street
Peterborough, N. H. 03458

WRITING STYLES: GRADE 3
INTRODUCTION

The Writing Process includes five stages:

Prewriting
Students think about topics, choose an idea, decide what kind of writing to do, make notes about the topic, and put the ideas in order.

Drafting
Students write quickly during this stage. They do not worry about mistakes.

Responding and Revising
Students read the writing to themselves or to partners. This is the stage to improve the writing.

Proofreading
Students read the writing again. They check to see that capitalization and punctuation are used correctly.

Publishing
Students share their writing with others.

This book is designed to give students practice in all stages of the writing process to help them become better writers.

ORGANIZATION OF UNIT
Each unit is organized to provide maximum practice in the writing process. Each unit begins with an assessment. Then, two lessons are provided for activities in the thinking, or *prewriting,* stage. Activities include connecting ideas in a sequence, connecting main idea and details, visualizing steps in a process, observing and classifying details, comparing and contrasting, drawing conclusions, and classifying fact and opinion.

The third lesson provides practice in the writer's craft. Activities include capturing the reader's interest, using enough details, writing for an audience and a purpose, using exact words for directions, using sensory words and vivid language, using dialogue, choosing words to paint a vivid picture, giving reasons, and using exact words.

The fourth type of lesson involves the practice of revising one's writing. Activities include using a thesaurus, keeping to the topic, joining sentences, combining sentences, avoiding run-on sentences, and expanding sentences.

The fifth type of lesson gives students practice proofreading.

Finally, each unit ends with three to five writing prompts for students to practice writing. Many of these are cooperative activities for students to do in pairs or in small groups.

ORGANIZATION OF BOOK
The book is organized into nine units that focus on the essential types of writing: personal narrative, information paragraph, friendly letter, how-to paragraph, descriptive paragraph, story, poem, persuasive paragraph, and research report.

A PERSONAL NARRATIVE
- *has one topic.*
- *tells about the writer.*
- *has sentences that tell what happens in the beginning, the middle, and the ending.*
- *uses the words* I, me, *and* my.

AN INFORMATION PARAGRAPH
- *tells about one main idea.*
- *has a topic sentence that tells the main idea.*
- *has detail sentences that tell facts about the main idea.*

A FRIENDLY LETTER

- *is a written message to a friend or a relative.*
- *has a heading, a greeting, a body, a closing, and a signature.*

A HOW-TO PARAGRAPH

- *tells how to do or make something.*
- *has a topic sentence.*
- *has detail sentences that tell what materials are needed.*
- *gives directions in order.*

A DESCRIPTIVE PARAGRAPH

- *tells what someone or something is like.*
- *paints a clear and vivid word picture.*

A STORY

- *has a title.*
- *has characters and a setting.*
- *has a problem that the characters must solve.*
- *has a beginning, a middle, and an ending.*

A POEM

- *tells a writer's feelings about a topic.*
- *can tell how things are alike and different.*
- *can have rhyming words.*

A PERSUASIVE PARAGRAPH

- *tells the writer's feelings.*
- *lists reasons.*
- *asks readers to agree with the writer.*

A RESEARCH REPORT

- *gives facts about one topic.*
- *usually has more than one paragraph.*
- *has a title that tells about the topic.*

USE

The activities in this book are designed for independent use by students who have had instruction in the specific skills covered in the lessons. Copies of the activity sheets can be given to individuals or pairs of students for completion. When students are familiar with the content of the worksheets, they can be assigned as homework.

To begin, determine the implementation that fits your students' needs and your classroom structure. The following plan suggests a format for this implementation.

1. **Administer** *the Assessment Test to establish baseline information on each student. This test may also be used as a post-test when the student has completed a unit.*

2. **Explain** *the purpose of the worksheets to the class.*

3. **Review** *the mechanics of how you want students to work with the activities. Do you want them to work in pairs? Are the activities for homework?*

4. **Introduce** *students to the process and purpose of the activities. Work with students when they have difficulty. Give them only a few pages at a time to avoid pressure.*

ADDITIONAL NOTES

1. **Parent Communication.** *Send the Letter to Parents home with students.*

2. **Bulletin Board.** *Display completed worksheets to show student progress.*

3. **Skills Correlation and Curriculum Correlation.** *These charts indicate specific skills incorporated in the activities to help you in your daily lesson planning.*

4. **Student Progress Chart.** *Duplicate the grid charts found on pages 7-8. Record student names in the left column. Note date of completion of each lesson for each student.*

Dear Parent:

During this school year, our class will be working on writing skills. We will be completing activity sheets that provide practice in the writing skills that can help your child become a better writer. The types of writing we will be focusing on are: personal narrative, information paragraph, friendly letter, how-to paragraph, descriptive paragraph, story, poem, persuasive paragraph, and research report.

From time to time, I may send home activity sheets. To best help your child, please consider the following suggestions:

- Provide a quiet place to work.
- Go over the directions together.
- Encourage your child to do his or her best.
- Check the lesson when it is complete.
- Go over your child's work, and note improvements as well as problems.

Help your child maintain a positive attitude about writing. Provide as many opportunities for your child to write as possible. Encourage your child to keep a Writer's Journal. A journal is like a diary. In it, your child can write about things that happen each day. Encourage your child to keep a running list of writing ideas. This can be a list of topics or story ideas for future writing projects. Display your child's writing and read the stories as a part of bedtime story time. Above all, enjoy this time you spend with your child. He or she will feel your support, and skills will improve with each activity completed.

Thank you for your help!

Cordially,

SKILLS CORRELATION

	Assessment	Thinking	Writer's Craft	Revising	Proofreading	Practice
Personal Narrative	9	10, 11	12	13	14	15, 16, 17
Information Paragraph	18	19, 20	21	22	23	24, 25, 26
Friendly Letter	27	28, 29	30	31	32	33, 34, 35
How-to Paragraph	36	37, 38	39	40	41	42, 43, 44, 45
Descriptive Paragraph	46	47, 48	49	50	51	52, 53, 54, 55, 56
Story	57	58, 59	60	61	62	63, 64, 65
Poem	66	67, 68	69		70	71, 72, 73
Persuasive Paragraph	74	75, 76	77	78	79	80, 81, 82, 83, 84
Research Report	85	86, 87	88	89	90	91, 92, 93, 94

CURRICULUM CORRELATION

	Social Studies	Science	Literature	Health	Physical Education	Art
Personal Narrative	14	9, 10, 11, 13, 16	12, 15			16
Information Paragraph	18, 20, 22	18, 19, 20, 21, 22, 23, 24, 26	25	22		24
Friendly Letter	27, 29, 30, 31, 32, 33, 34, 35	29, 30, 31				
How-to Paragraph	38, 40, 42, 43, 45	37, 40, 41, 43, 44, 45		37, 38, 43, 44		36, 39, 43
Descriptive Paragraph	46, 47, 49, 51, 52, 55	48, 50, 51, 53, 54, 56	46, 47, 49			52, 53, 54, 55, 56
Story	61, 63	57, 65	57, 58, 59, 60, 62, 64, 65, 66	58, 60	63	64
Poem	67, 72	71, 72, 73	69, 70	67		73
Persuasive Paragraph	76, 77, 78, 79, 80, 81, 82, 83, 84	74, 75, 80	79, 83	75	75, 78	80, 83
Research Report	85, 87, 90	85, 86, 87, 88, 89, 90, 91, 92, 93, 94		86		91, 92, 93

STUDENT PROGRESS CHART

Student Name	Unit 1 Personal Narrative								Unit 2 Information								Unit 3 Friendly Letter								Unit 4 How-To									Unit 5 Descriptive									
	1	2	3	4	5	6	7	8	1	2	3	4	5	6	7	8	1	2	3	4	5	6	7	8	1	2	3	4	5	6	7	8	9	1	2	3	4	5	6	7	8	9	10

STUDENT PROGRESS CHART

Student Name	Unit 6 Story								Unit 7 Poem							Unit 8 Persuasive										Unit 9 Research									Comments
	1	2	3	4	5	6	7	8	1	2	3	4	5	6	7	1	2	3	4	5	6	7	8	9	10	1	2	3	4	5	6	7	8	9	

Writing Styles 3, SV 8056-1

Name _____ Date _____

UNIT 1: Personal Narrative
Assessment

Read the three sentences. Label each one *beginning, middle,* or *ending.*

1. A patch of lettuce grew under my window.

   _____

2. I planted seeds under my window.

   _____

3. Mom picked the lettuce for a salad.

   _____

Choose the title you think is more interesting. Draw a line under it. Write a sentence to tell why you think so.

4. A Black Dog   The Tallest Dog in the World

Write a story about how you got to school today.

_____

_____

_____

_____

_____

Name _____ Date _____

Analyzing a Personal Narrative

A personal narrative
- *has one topic.*
- *tells about the writer.*
- *has sentences that tell what happens in the beginning, the middle, and the ending.*
- *uses the words* I, me, *and* my.

Read each group of sentences. Label each one *beginning, middle,* or *ending.*

1. I put my palm tree near a window.

   _____

2. I bought a potted palm tree at the plant store.

   _____

3. I brought the palm tree home.

   _____

4. After reading that, I took my palm tree into the shower with me.

   _____

5. The book said that palm trees should be washed often.

   _____

6. I read about palm trees in a book about plants.

   _____

Connecting Ideas in a Sequence

✎ *To write a personal narrative, good writers*
   • *tell about things in the order in which they happen.*

Read each paragraph. Then number the events below it in the order in which they happened.

1. We looked at the four eggs on the leaves of the tomato plant. They were about as big as the head of a pin. During the week, we watched as the pale green eggs changed to yellowish-green and then almost white. One morning something inside started to cut a hole in one of the eggs. Soon a tiny caterpillar crawled out of the egg. Within a short time, all the eggs had hatched.

   _____ The eggs changed to yellowish-green, then white.

   _____ The eggs hatched.

   _____ We saw pale green eggs on the tomato leaves.

2. The first thing the pale caterpillars did was start to eat tomato leaves. We watched as they grew and grew. After a few days, the skin of each one split down the back. Each caterpillar crawled out of the old skin. There was a new, bigger skin underneath. Each caterpillar was about four inches long and bright green in color.

   _____ The caterpillars began to eat the tomato leaves.

   _____ The caterpillars were four inches long and bright green.

   _____ The skin of the caterpillars split for the first time.

Capturing the Reader's Interest

> *Good writers capture the reader's interest by creating*
> - *a catchy title.*
>   - *a strong beginning sentence.*

Choose the title you think is more interesting. Draw a line under it. Write a sentence to tell why you think so.

1. Mysteries, Monsters, and Untold Secrets   Things We Don't Understand

   _____

2. Jim Saves Time   A Wrinkle in Time

   _____

3. The No-Return Trail   The Country Road

   _____

4. From the Mixed-Up Files of Mrs. Basil E. Frankenweiler   The Day I Ran Away from Home

   _____

5. Willie Bea's Day   Willie Bea and the Day the Martians Landed

   _____

Using the Thesaurus

- *A thesaurus is a book of* synonyms, *or words that have nearly the same meaning.*
- Antonyms, *words that mean the opposite of the entry word, follow the synonyms.*

Replace the underlined word with a synonym or antonym. Use a thesaurus or a dictionary to find synonyms and antonyms. Write the new word on the line.

1. Dan will <u>get</u> a baby duck in the spring.

   synonym--- _____

2. Dan is very <u>lucky</u>.

   synonym--- _____

3. A baby deer would make a <u>good</u> pet.

   antonym--- _____

4. Pets <u>need</u> special food and water.

   synonym--- _____

5. It is best not to <u>purchase</u> a pet you can't keep.

   synonym--- _____

6. Baby raccoons are the <u>most</u> popular wild animal pets.

   antonym--- _____

7. It is very <u>kind</u> to keep raccoons in a cage.

   antonym--- _____

Proofreading a Personal Narrative

PROOFREADING HINT
To be a good proofreader, look for one type of error at a time.
For example, proofread once for capitalization errors, once
for punctuation errors, and once for spelling errors.

Proofread the beginning of the personal narrative, paying special attention to end marks. Use the Proofreader's Marks to correct at least seven errors.

Uncle John has always been my favorite uncle What a surprise we all had last summer Late one evening there was a knock at the back door. Can you guess who was standing on our back steps Of course, it was Uncle John He had a backpack, a small suitcase, and an armload of gifts.

Proofreader's Marks
≡ Use a capital letter.
⊙ Add a period.
∧ Add something.
⋏ Add a comma.
˅˅ Add quotation marks.
✄ Cut something.
⋏ Replace something.
∿ Transpose.
◯ Spell correctly.
⌁ Indent paragraph.
/ Make a lowercase letter.

Uncle John's present for me was a bright blew T-shirt. it has a picture of an old castle on the back. Uncle John bought the shirt for me when he was traveling in England last year I wore that shirt every day wile Uncle John was staying with us

Uncle John has been to many different parts of the world, and he loved telling us about his adventures. Listening to his stories was almost as much fun as going along on Uncle John's trips

Order a Story

With a small group, write eight sentences of a story on each of the boxes on this page. Cut out the boxes. Trade cards with another group. Working together, put the sentences in order. Read the story aloud to see if it makes sense.

Unit 1: Personal Narrative
Writing Styles 3, SV 8056-1

Write Your Own Sentences

Pick your favorite kind of dinosaur. Draw a picture of that dinosaur. Under the picture write three sentences that tell about it.

_____

_____

_____

_____

_____

_____

Name _____ Date _____

Write About Wishes

Talk with a friend about wishes. Make a list of your wishes.

_____   _____

_____   _____

_____   _____

_____   _____

Write four sentences about your wishes. Be sure to revise and proofread your sentences.

_____

_____

_____

_____

_____

_____

Unit 1: Personal Narrative
Writing Styles 3, SV 8056-1

UNIT 2: Information Paragraph
Assessment

Read the paragraph. Draw a line under the sentence that tells the main idea. Then list two details.

Animal tracks can tell you many things. For example, most cat tracks are smaller than dog tracks. Also, cat tracks are more rounded than dog tracks are. Cats usually keep their nails pulled in, but dogs can't do that. So dog tracks show nail marks.

1. _____

2. _____

Read each paragraph. Answer the questions.

A. People who live in cities enjoy parks. Many families spend the day in the park. They do many fun things. Sometimes they have a picnic lunch.

B. People who live in cities enjoy parks. Many families spend the entire day in the park. They begin the morning with a canoe ride on the deep, blue lake. Ducks and turtles watch the canoes go by. At noon, they stop for a picnic of chicken, fruit, and cake. The family spends the afternoon looking for bears, elephants, and dragons in the clouds.

3. Which paragraph is more interesting? Explain your answer.

_____

4. What is one detail given in the second paragraph?

_____

Analyzing an Information Paragraph

> **An information paragraph**
> - *is a group of sentences.*
> - *tells about one main idea.*
> - *has a topic sentence that tells the main idea.*
> - *has detail sentences that tell facts about the main idea.*

Read each paragraph. Draw a line under the sentence that tells the main idea. Then list two details.

1. The squid and the octopus look very different. The octopus has a round head and body. It has eight arms, or tentacles, on the bottom of its body. The squid is torpedo-shaped. All its tentacles are at one end. Eight of them are the same length. Two are longer, for a total of ten.

   a. _____

   b. _____

2. The squid and the octopus behave very differently. The squid can shoot through the water at great speed. The octopus moves more slowly and spends most of its time on the sea bottom.

   a. _____

   b. _____

Name _____ Date _____

Connecting Main Idea and Details

To write an information paragraph, good writers
- *think about one main idea.*
  - *plan interesting details to tell about the main idea.*

Read each group of sentences. Write *main idea* or *detail* to tell what each would be in a paragraph.

1. a. If you break off the end, you can make an herb pot.

   _____

   b. You can arrange cracked pieces into a design.

   _____

   c. A person can do a lot of things with an eggshell.

   _____

   d. You can decorate it for certain holidays.

   _____

2. a. Place the egg over a bowl.

   _____

   b. With a safety pin make a small hole in each end of a raw egg.

   _____

   c. Slowly run water through the hollow egg to clean it out.

   _____

   d. It is easy to hollow out an egg.

   _____

Name _____ Date _____

Using Enough Details

> ✏️ *Good writers give readers*
> - *interesting details.*
> - *clear examples.*

Read each paragraph. Answer the questions.

Owls are best known for their ability to see at night. They can see 100 times better than humans. Their eyes are big and do not move very easily. This is why owls' necks have to turn so far.

Though they can also see well in the daytime, owls are known for seeing at night. They can see 100 times better at night than humans can, but they are color-blind. Owls' eyes are very large, and they control the light coming in by changing the size of the pupil of the eyes. Each pupil acts alone. If you stood in the sun and your friend stood in the shade, an owl could see each of you well.

1. Which paragraph is more interesting? Explain your answer.

   _____

2. What is one detail given in the second paragraph?

   _____

3. Write one example found in the second paragraph.

   _____

Keeping to the Topic

> ✏️ • *A good writer plans a paragraph so that it shares details about one main idea.*
>   • *All the sentences in a paragraph must keep to the topic.*

Read the topic sentence below. Choose the sentences that keep to the topic. Write a paragraph, using the topic sentence and the sentences you chose.

<u>A sighted person can only imagine what it is like to be blind</u>.
Put a scarf over your eyes to block out light.
Try to figure out what different foods are.
Being deaf is not easy either.
Pretend to pay for something with coins.
Try to walk into another room and sit at a table.
A person who cannot hear has different problems.
Blind people can do all these things and more.

Name ______________________________ Date ______________________________

Proofreading an Information Paragraph

PROOFREADING HINT

To be a good proofreader, look for one type of error at a time. For example, proofread once for capitalization errors, once for punctuation errors, and once for spelling errors.

Proofread the information paragraphs, paying special attention to missing words. Use the Proofreader's Marks to correct at least six errors.

Proofreader's Marks

- ≡ Use a capital letter.
- ⊙ Add a period.
- ∧ Add something.
- ∧ Add a comma.
- ∨∨ Add quotation marks.
- Cut something.
- Replace something.
- Transpose.
- ○ Spell correctly.
- ¶ Indent paragraph.
- / Make a lowercase letter.

Pond snails are useful in fish tanks. Pond snails will any extra food your fish leave. They will also eat some the moss that appears on the plants. The snails will eat some of moss on the glass walls of the tank, too If you have sevrel pond snails in fish tank, you will not have to clean the tank as often.

If your pond snails are having babies, be sure to remove the snails the tank. Fish will eat snail eggs. In the same way, if your fish are having babies, be sure remove the snails. Snails will eat fish eggs.

There are many different kinds snails. Their different kinds shells can add grately to the beauty of your fish tank. Not only are snails useful in keeping a tank clean, they also add interest to the tank.

Name _____ Date _____

Write About Zoo Animals

With a partner, choose one animal you
would like to see at the zoo. Draw a
picture of the animal. Then write four
sentences about the animal. You
might write about the animal's looks,
food, and special needs.

_____

_____

_____

_____

_____

_____

_____

Name _____ Date _____

Make a List and Write a Paragraph

With a partner, make a list of ten interesting topics to write about. Then work alone to pick one of the topics for your paragraph. Write the paragraph. Add one sentence that does not keep to your topic. Exchange papers with your partner. Read his or her paragraph and draw a line through the sentence that does not belong. Compare your answers.

Name _____ Date _____

Write About Farm Animals

With a partner, write a paragraph about your favorite farm animals. Tell what those animals eat and do. Proofread and revise your paragraph.

_____

_____

_____

_____

_____

_____

_____

_____

_____

_____

Name _____ Date _____

UNIT 3: Friendly Letter
Assessment

Draw a line under the correct answer.

1. How does a friendly letter close?
   a. with the greeting   b. with a signature
   c. with the body of the letter

2. What does the body in a friendly letter do?
   a. It tells the message.   b. It says good-bye.
   c. It tells the writer's address and the date.

Read the letter. Write an answer to each question.

324 Sunshine Drive
San Antonio, TX 78211
October 8, 1998

Dear Aunt Margaret,
    I received the shirt you sent today. It is so pretty. Blue is my favorite color. I am going to wear it to school tomorrow. Thank you very much.
    I can't wait to see you in December.

Much love,
Rosa

3. What is the purpose for writing?

_____

4. When was the letter written? How do you know?

_____

5. Who wrote the letter? How do you know?

_____

Name _____ Date _____

Analyzing a Friendly Letter

A friendly letter
- *is a written message to a friend or a relative.*
- *has a heading, a greeting, a body, a closing, and a signature.*

A. Write each letter part correctly.

1. 486 amigo Avenue _____

   San diego, California 92116 _____

   april 14 1999 _____

2. Dear roberto _____

3. your friend _____

4. Your Cousin, _____

5. dear alice, _____

B. Draw a line under the correct answer.

6. What does the closing in a friendly letter do?
   a. It says hello.
   b. It says good-bye.
   c. It tells the writer's name.

7. What does the body in a friendly letter do?
   a. It tells the writer's address and the date.
   b. It tells the writer's name.
   c. It tells the message.

8. What does the greeting do?
   a. It says good-bye.
   b. It tells the message.
   c. It says hello.

Connecting Ideas In a Summary

To write a friendly letter, good writers
- *include interesting details.*
  - *pull together ideas to use fewer words.*

Read each group of sentences. Write *detail* or *summary* to tell what each sentence is.

1. a. Skip has red hair like his dad's. _____

   b. Skip's long, straight nose looks just like his mom's.

   _____

   c. Skip looks a lot like his parents. _____

   d. Skip has long fingers like his mom's. _____

   e. Skip and his dad are both of average height. _____

2. a. Some apples are green. _____

   b. Some apples are large. _____

   c. Some apples are red. _____

   d. Apples come in many sizes, shapes, and colors. _____

   e. Some apples are rounder than others. _____

Writing for an Audience and a Purpose

Good writers
- *have a purpose for writing.*
  - *choose an audience.*
    - *think of ideas that will interest the audience.*

Read the letter. Write an answer to each question.

859 Oak Street
Pasadena, CA 91107
May 14, 1998

Dear Grandma and Grandpa,
  I had a good time when I visited you last week. I thought you would like to know that I did a report on farm life. I talked to my class about milking cows. I told the class that you showed me how to do it. How is the new calf?

  See you next month.

  Lots of love,
  Mimi

1. What is the purpose for writing?

  _____

  _____

2. Who is the audience? How do you know?

  _____

  _____

3. Who wrote the letter? How do you know?

  _____

  _____

Name _____ Date _____

Joining Sentences

✏️ • *Good writers make their writing more interesting by joining sentences that are short and choppy.*
• *Sentences that have ideas that go together can be joined with a comma (,) and the word* and.

Use a comma and the word *and* to join each pair of sentences. Write a new sentence.

1. Inventions make our lives easier. We take them for granted.

   _____

   _____

2. We get cold. We turn on a heater.

   _____

   _____

3. Long ago people got cold. They sat around a fire.

   _____

   _____

4. A very long time ago, people had no fire. They stayed cold.

   _____

   _____

5. Our heater works. We stay warm.

   _____

   _____

Proofreading a Friendly Letter

PROOFREADING HINT
To be a good proofreader, look for one type of error at a time. For example, proofread once for capitalization errors, once for punctuation errors, and once for spelling errors.

Proofread the friendly letters, paying special attention to capital letters and commas. Use the Proofreader's Marks to correct at least eight errors.

Proofreader's Marks

≡ Use a capital letter.
⊙ Add a period.
∧ Add something.
⋏ Add a comma.
ⱽⱽ Add quotation marks.
✄ Cut something.
⋏ Replace something.
⁀ Transpose.
◯ Spell correctly.
⊞ Indent paragraph.
/ Make a lowercase letter.

1632 Moorish road
Garden Grove California 92640
march 14, 1998

dear Uncle Olaf
    We got a new baby last week. Her name is Katrina. We were so lucky to adopt her. What small fingers she has Her grip is very strong. I think I like being a brother.

your nephew
Hans

4622 glen Road
bonnie Doon, California 95060
March 28, 1998

Dear hans,
    Thanx for telling me about Katrina. I am looking forward to visiting you in April. You can show me just how strong Katrina's grip is.

love
Uncle Olaf

Write a Letter to a Classmate

In a group, put each person's name on a piece of paper and put the papers in a box. Each person picks one name from the box. Write to the person whose name you chose. Be sure to write about things that would interest the person.

Dear _____,

Name _____ Date _____

A Friendly Letter

Think about who would enjoy a letter from you. Fill in this chart to help you find what message you want to share.

Whom I'm writing to:

_____

_____

Where my reader lives:

_____

_____

What my reader likes to do:

_____

_____

A pet or other animal my reader likes:

_____

_____

Now, write the three-sentence letter.

_____

_____

_____

_____

_____

_____

_____

_____

_____

Write a Letter to a Family Member

 Here are some questions to help you decide what to write in the body of your friendly letter.

Write your ideas about the questions below. Then write a friendly letter to a family member.

What important news could you share?

How would you ask your family member what's new?

What other message would you like to share?

_____

_____

_____

_____

_____

_____

_____

_____

Name _____ Date _____

UNIT 4: How-to Paragraph
Assessment

Read the how-to paragraph. Answer the questions that follow.

To tie-dye a shirt, start by bunching a white shirt in a ball and wrapping rubber bands tightly around it. Or, you might want to fold it back and forth like a fan and then wrap rubber bands around it. Next, soak the shirt in clear water. Then place it in the dye. Let it soak for a few minutes. Remove from the dye and rinse it until the water runs clear. Remove some of the rubber bands and put it in another color of dye. Finally, remove all the rubber bands to see your brightly-colored, tie-dyed shirt.

1. What does this how-to paragraph teach?

   _____

   _____

   _____

2. List at least two words or phrases that tell time order.

   _____

   _____

   _____

3. What is the last step?

   _____

   _____

   _____

Analyzing a How-to Paragraph

A how-to paragraph
- *tells how to do or make something.*
- *has a topic sentence.*
- *has detail sentences that tell what materials are needed.*
- *gives directions in order.*

Read the how-to paragraph. Answer the questions that follow.

To cook a fried egg, you will need the following things: an egg, a tablespoon of butter, a frying pan with a cover, a teaspoon of water, and a spatula. The first thing you do is melt the butter in the pan over medium heat. Do not let the butter turn brown. After that, break the egg against the edge of the pan and gently pour the egg into the pan. Throw away the shell. Let the egg cook for about a minute. Then, sprinkle about a teaspoon of water into the frying pan cover and place it over the pan. Lower the heat and cook for another minute, or until the egg looks firm and there is a thin film over the yolk. Finally, use a spatula to remove the egg from the pan.

1. What does this how-to paragraph teach?

_____

2. What materials are needed?

_____

3. List at least three words or phrases that tell time order.

_____

4. What different time-order word or phrase could have been used in the fourth sentence?

_____

Name _____ Date _____

Visualizing Steps in a Process

To write a how-to paragraph, good writers
  • make a "movie" in their minds showing the steps of an
    activity.
    • write the steps in the order in which they "see" them.

**A. Read the directions. As you read, try
to visualize the steps. Then write the
step or steps that were left out.**

1. Pick up your toothbrush.
   Open your mouth and put the toothbrush in it.
   Brush teeth with an up-and-down motion.
   Take toothbrush out of your mouth.
   Rinse toothpaste out of your mouth.

   _____

2. Enter library.
   Find books.
   Carry books out.
   Walk home.

   _____

B. Read the steps. Number them in order.

_____ Put food in dish.

_____ Open can of cat food.

_____ Place dish of food on floor for cat.

_____ Remove can of cat food from cabinet.

Using Exact Words for Directions

✏ *Good writers*   • *use time-order words to tell the steps in order.*

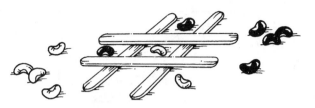

Read the paragraph. Answer the questions that follow.

How to Make a Tic-Tac-Toe Game

The first thing you need to do is get four popsicle sticks and find some white glue. Then, place two sticks beside each other about 1 1/2 inches apart. Next, glue the other sticks across the first two. After that, allow the glue to dry. The last thing you do is get six light-colored beans and six dark-colored ones. To play tic-tac-toe, use the beans as markers.

1. What is the first thing you do?

   _____

   _____

2. What is the last step before playing the game?

   _____

   _____

3. What words or phrases give you clues about the time order?

   _____

   _____

4. What different time-order word or phrase could have been used in place of *Then*?

   _____

   _____

Name _____ Date _____

Joining Sentences to List Words in a Series

> ✏ • *A list of three or more materials or items is called a series.*
> • *Short, choppy sentences can be combined into one long,*
>   *clear sentence with a series.*

Join each pair of sentences. Write the new sentence.

1. Pet mice can be black. They can be red or silver.

   _____

   _____

2. Other colors for mice include gray. They also include cream and white.

   _____

   _____

3. A mouse can chew on wood. It can chew on nuts and twigs.

   _____

   _____

4. Mice clean their own bodies. They clean their faces and ears.

   _____

   _____

5. Soup cans are good resting places for pet mice. They are good for hamsters and gerbils, too.

   _____

   _____

Proofreading a How-to Paragraph

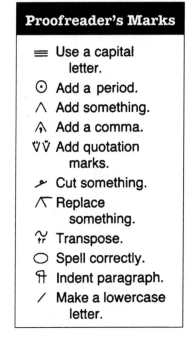

PROOFREADING HINT
To be a good proofreader, look for one type of error at a time.
For example, proofread once for capitalization errors, once
for punctuation errors, and once for spelling errors.

Proofread the how-to paragraphs, paying special attention to commas. Use the Proofreader's Marks to correct at least seven errors.

You can create a garden in a bottle. You will need some planting tools a bottle and some soil. You'll also need charcoal, pebbles and plants. For a small garden, use any one-gallon bottle. For a larger garden, use a five-gallon watter bottle. To begin, make a funnel that will reach to the bottom of your bottle. You can do this by twisting a peace of stiff paper or aluminum foil into a cone shape Use this funnel to guide each set of materials into the bottle.

First, put a layer of pebbles at least one inch thick into the bottle. The pebbles will absorb water. This will help prevent root rot, fungus and other plant problems. Next, add about two inches of clean soil Then, use a stick a pencil or a chopstick to make a hole for each plant in your bottle garden.

Proofreader's Marks

≡ Use a capital letter.
⊙ Add a period.
∧ Add something.
⩕ Add a comma.
ᵛⱽ Add quotation marks.
⤴ Cut something.
⋀ Replace something.
ᴎ Transpose.
◯ Spell correctly.
Ⴕ Indent paragraph.
/ Make a lowercase letter.

Name _____ Date _____

Write About a Game

Talk with another student about games you both like to play. List them. Together, write at least four sentences telling how to play one of the games.

Games We Like to Play

_____

_____

_____

_____

_____

How to Play

_____

_____

_____

_____

_____

_____

_____

_____

_____

Write About Cooking

With a partner, decide on a food you would like to cook. Together, write a short paragraph about making that food. Then, draw a picture of the finished product.

How to Make

_____

_____

_____

_____

_____

_____

_____

Name _____ Date _____

Write a Recipe

With a small group list all the things you like to eat in a salad. Then write four sentences telling how to make a salad.

_____   _____

_____   _____

_____   _____

_____   _____

Salad

_____

_____

_____

_____

_____

_____

_____

Write About Taking Care of a Pet

With a small group, list pets you own or would like to own.

_____   _____

_____   _____

_____   _____

_____   _____

Then choose one pet from the list and together write five sentences about how to care for the pet.

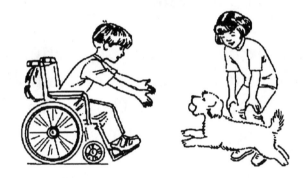

_____

_____

_____

_____

_____

_____

_____

UNIT 5: Descriptive Paragraph
Assessment

Read each paragraph. Underline the correct answer for each numbered sentence.

Lori picked up Casey's right leg and put it into the green pants. Casey squirmed and his leg came out of the pants.

"Do you not like those green pants?" Lori asked. She picked up the red and white striped pants. Casey lay still while Lori put the pants on him.

Then Lori picked up the blue hat with a red ball on top. She tied the hat under Casey's chin. Casey shook his head. Lori pulled Casey's tail out of the hole she'd cut in the pants.

"You look cute, Casey!" Lori said.

Casey said, "Meow."

1. What color pants would Casey not wear?
   a. green
   b. red and white striped
   c. blue

2. How did Lori make the pants fit Casey?
   a. She picked the pair that fit the best.
   b. She picked the pair Casey liked the best.
   c. She cut a hole for Casey's tail.

3. What two details tell you Casey is a cat?

   _____

   _____

   _____

Name _____ Date _____

Analyzing a Descriptive Paragraph

A descriptive paragraph
- *tells what someone or something is like.*
- *paints a clear and vivid word picture.*

A. Read each sentence. Write the words that describe colors, shapes, and sizes.

1. Juanita bought a thick red blanket. _____

2. She carried it home in a round basket. _____

3. Her green basket had an orange pattern in it.

   _____

4. As she got close to her two-story house, her tiny puppy

   greeted her. _____

5. "Hi, Zorba, you huge hound!" Juanita said. _____

6. Juanita spoiled her little brown dog. _____

7. The colorful blanket was for Zorba. _____

B. Read each sentence. Write the words that describe sounds, tastes, smells, and feelings.

8. A loud banging sound came from the kitchen.

   _____

9. "What a terrific smell!" Juanita thought. _____

10. "Dad is baking another delicious pie," she said. _____

11. "It must be a spicy, tender pie," she said. _____

Name _____ Date _____

Observing Details

✎ *To write a descriptive paragraph, good writers*
  • pay close attention to what they will describe.

Read each paragraph. Underline the correct ending for each numbered sentence.

The cactus wren is the largest member of the wren family. Its back is brown with black bars and white streaks. There is a white stripe over each eye. The bird's breast is white, spotted with black.

1. The details in this
   paragraph tell
   a. about the bird's nest.
   b. about the bird's coloring.
   c. about the bird's life.

2. The colors of the
   cactus wren are
   a. black and white.
   b. brown and white.
   c. black, brown, and white.

The California poppy is sometimes called the golden poppy. It is a bright yellow color, shading to gold at its center. The flower is two or three inches across. The plant grows two feet tall. In the spring countless millions of these plants cover California's mountainsides with gold.

3. The details in this
   paragraph tell
   a. about the poppy's color
      and size.
   b. about California's ocean.
   c. about California's weather.

4. What name does
   this plant not have?
   a. golden poppy
   b. mountainside poppy
   c. California poppy

Using Sensory Words and Vivid Language

Good writers
- *use sensory words to tell how someone or something looks, feels, sounds, smells, or tastes.*
  - *use exact verbs to tell how someone or something moves.*

Read each sentence. Decide which one of the senses is being used. Write *look, feel, sound, taste,* or *smell* on the line.

1. The chimneys were outlined against a pale, pink sky.

   _____

2. The morning air was very chilly. _____

3. Suddenly a loud cry broke the silence. _____

4. A young boy poked his head out of one chimney.

   _____

5. The boy called "All up!" in a loud voice.

   _____

6. He waved his cleaning tools.

   _____

7. Then he slid into the chimney to clean it. _____

8. Later he had some spicy cider to drink. _____

9. He warmed his hands on the hot cup. _____

10. The smell of roast pork filled the air. _____

49

Name _____ Date _____

Combining Sentences

- *Good writers often combine short sentences to make writing interesting.*
- *Two sentences might have the same predicate. The sentences can be combined by joining the subjects with the word* and.

Combine each pair of sentences into one sentence. Remember to join subjects with the word *and*. Write the new sentence.

1. Guppies are pets for fish tanks. Goldfish are pets for fish tanks.

   _____

   _____

2. Catfish clean harmful moss from the tank. Snails clean harmful moss from the tank.

   _____

   _____

3. Black mollies are lovely fish. Goldfish are lovely fish.

   _____

   _____

4. Guppies have live babies. Black mollies have live babies.

   _____

   _____

5. Zebra fish lay eggs. Angelfish lay eggs.

   _____

Observing Details

PROOFREADING HINT
To be a good proofreader, look for one type of error at a time.
For example, proofread once for capitalization errors, once
for punctuation errors, and once for spelling errors.

Proofread the descriptive paragraphs, paying special attention to the verbs that go with sentence subjects. Use the Proofreader's Marks to correct at least seven errors.

Have you ever heard of a person who likes washing dishes? My friend Dan really enjoy it. In fact, Dan washes dishes whenever he can. Dan pull a chair over to the sink so he can reach everything easily. Dan likes the lemony smell of the liquid detergent He squeezes the bottle gently and watches the liquid soap stream into the water. The soap mix with the hot water. Together, they create a mass of frothy white bubbles. When the bubbles almost reach the top of the sink, Dan turns the water off. then he carefully puts the glasses into the water.

Proofreader's Marks

≡ Use a capital letter.
⊙ Add a period.
∧ Add something.
⋏ Add a comma.
Ꮩ Ꮩ Add quotation marks.
✄ Cut something.
⋏ Replace something.
∿ Transpose.
◯ Spell correctly.
⏀ Indent paragraph.
/ Make a lowercase letter.

Most of all, Dan like using a brand-new dishcloth. The cloth feel soft in Dan's hands. It has a clean smell, too. Dan rub each glass carefully with the soft, new cloth. Then he rinses the glass and sets it on the drainer.

Name _____ Date _____

Write About a Holiday

With a partner, choose one special holiday. Draw a picture of the holiday celebration. Write at least four sentences about it. Tell why you like the holiday and what you enjoy doing on the holiday.

_____

_____

_____

_____

_____

_____

Name _____ Date _____

Write About the Weather

With a partner, choose your favorite kind of weather. Draw a picture showing that weather. Then write four sentences to describe your picture.

_____

_____

_____

_____

_____

Unit 5: Descriptive Paragraph
Writing Styles 3, SV 8056-1

Name _____ Date _____

Write About Food

Look through old magazines or newspapers and cut out pictures of food. Paste each picture on this page. Write sentences to describe each food.

Describe a Friend

Work with a partner. Look closely at your partner, observing at least five attractive details about him or her. Write five details that your partner would be happy to hear. Draw a picture of your partner. Exchange papers and read details about yourself.

My Friend

_____

_____

_____

_____

_____

_____

_____

_____

_____

_____

_____

_____

_____

Name _____ Date _____

Write About a Pet

With a small group, draw a picture of a pet.
Write three sentences describing the pet.

Name _____ Date _____

UNIT 6: Story
Assessment

Read the story. Answer the questions that follow.

Pet Day at School

Yesterday we brought our pets to school. They made a lot of noise.

Mr. McGrath said, "Quiet down, dogs! Lie down, cats!"

We tried to help Mr. McGrath. My big dog got excited. She barked and barked. One cat scratched Jose's little dog. Even the ferret was making noise! Jenny didn't have any trouble with her pets. She had three big goldfish.

"You have wonderful pets, Jenny," Mr. McGrath said.

Finally, we all took our pets outside. Except Jenny, of course!

1. What is the setting for this story?

   _____

2. What is the problem Mr. McGrath must solve?

   _____

3. What kind of person is Mr. McGrath?
   a. unhappy
   b. silly
   c. a dog lover

4. Why didn't Jenny's pets cause problems?
   a. Jenny didn't bring any pets.
   b. Fish don't make noise.
   c. Jenny took them outside.

Analyzing a Story

A story has
- *a title.*
- *characters and a setting.*
- *a problem that the characters must solve.*
- *a beginning, a middle, and an ending.*

Read the story. Answer the questions that follow.

King Midas was a kind but silly man who lived in Greece long ago. One day, in exchange for a kindness, he was granted a wish. Without thinking, King Midas asked that everything he touched would turn to gold. The "golden touch," as it was called, made him very rich. Even his food and drink turned to gold. Midas could not eat or drink. The worst thing was what happened when his daughter ran to hug him. She, too, turned to gold. Finally King Midas had to beg to have his golden touch taken away.

1. Who is the main character?

   _____

2. What is the setting?

   _____

3. What is the problem the character must solve?

   _____

   _____

4. Write one sentence that tells the middle.

   _____

5. Write one sentence that tells the ending.

   _____

Classifying Details as Real or Make-Believe

> ✏️ *To write a make-believe story, good writers*
> * *use both real and make-believe details.*

A. Read the paragraph. Then write three details that are real and three that are make-believe.

Alice sat by the stream with her sister. Just then a white rabbit ran by. The rabbit took a watch out of its vest pocket. It looked at the watch and declared, "I'm late!" Then the rabbit went down a hole in the ground.

Real

1. _____

2. _____

3. _____

Make-Believe

4. _____

5. _____

6. _____

B. Write *real* or *make-believe* on the line.

7. Alice walked in a garden. _____

8. She saw a caterpillar on a leaf. _____

9. The caterpillar asked, "Who are you?" _____

10. The Queen was a playing card. _____

Storytelling - Dialogue and Characters

> ❝ *Good writers use dialogue*
> *• to tell what each character is saying.*
>   *• to show what each character is like.*
>   *• to show how a character feels.*

Read the story with dialogue. Draw a line under the best answer to each question that follows.

"How do you feel?" asked the nurse, looking at the little boy in his hospital bed.

"My ear hurts," the boy answered sadly.

"Does it hurt a lot?" asked the nurse.

"Yes, but I can take it," answered the boy.

The nurse had known children like this before. The child, trying to be brave, would not say how much a pain hurts. The nurse had a special chart for children like this. It showed a ladder. The bottom rung of the ladder meant very little pain, and the top rung meant a lot. The nurse showed her chart to the boy.

"I'm on rung three," said the child, pointing to the middle of the ladder.

"Tell me when you're on rung four," said the nurse, smiling at him. "Then I'll give you some medicine for pain."

1. Who does the talking in this story?

   a. a nurse and a little boy   b. a nurse   c. a boy

2. What kind of person is the nurse?

   a. mean   b. kind   c. silly

3. What kind of person is the boy?

   a. active   b. cruel   c. brave

4. Who says, "I'm on rung three"?

   a. the doctor   b. the nurse   c. the boy

Avoiding Run-on Sentences

> ✏️ • *Good writers divide run-on sentences into two or more sentences.*

Revise each run-on sentence. Write two shorter sentences to make the meaning clearer.

1. The baby opened the cabinet she took out all the pots.

   _____

   _____

2. The mother came into the kitchen she saw the mess.

   _____

   _____

3. The mother smiled at the baby she asked if it was fun.

   _____

   _____

4. The baby smiled back she was having a good time.

   _____

   _____

5. The mother sat on the floor she played with the baby.

   _____

   _____

Name _____ Date _____

Proofreading a Story

PROOFREADING HINT
To be a good proofreader, look for one type of error at a time. For example, proofread once for capitalization errors, once for punctuation errors, and once for spelling errors.

Proofread the stories, paying special attention to capital letters at the beginning of sentences. Use the Proofreader's Marks to correct at least six errors.

1. Fox looked up at the grapes on the vine. how delicious they looked! he decided to have some grapes four his lunch. The grapes were quite high, and it was hard for Fox to reach them. he stretched and jumped, but he couldn't get the grapes. Fox tried again and again. the grapes always seemed just out of reach. Finally, Fox gave up. he walked away, asking himself, "Who would want those sour old grapes?"

Proofreader's Marks
≡ Use a capital letter.
⊙ Add a period.
∧ Add something.
⋏ Add a comma.
ⱽⱽ Add quotation marks.
✂ Cut something.
⋀ Replace something.
∿ Transpose.
◯ Spell correctly.
⁋ Indent paragraph.
/ Make a lowercase letter.

2. Goldilocks sat down at the bears' table. the first chair she tried was too hard, and the second chair was too soft. the third chair felt just right. Next, Goldilocks tried all the oatmeal on the table The first bowl was too hot, and the second bowl was too cold. The third bowl tasted just right. after she had eaten the whole bowl of oatmeal, Goldilocks went upstairs for a nap.

Unit 6: Story
© Steck-Vaughn Company
62
Writing Styles 3, SV 8056-1

Name _____ Date _____

Write a Story

What might happen when a group of friends go skating? With three or four other students, plan and write a story about a skating party.

Ideas for story

_____   _____

_____   _____

_____   _____

_____

The Skating Party

_____

_____

_____

_____

_____

_____

_____

_____

_____

_____

_____

_____

Name _____ Date _____

Write an Animal Story

With another student, imagine that some mice and some geese become friends. Write three sentences telling what the animals will do. Draw a picture to go with your story.

_____

_____

_____

_____

_____

Write a Story for Younger Children

All kinds of animals make good stories. Here are some animals you may want to write about. Some are real. Some are make-believe. They may make great characters for your story. Add more animals to each list.

pony

raccoon

a frog that sings

a pet rhinoceros

Pick one of the animals from the list. Write a make-believe story about that animal to entertain younger children.

_____

_____

_____

_____

_____

_____

Name _____ Date _____

UNIT 7: Poem
Assessment

Read the poem and the questions that follow. Underline the correct answer to each question.

Hickory Dickory Dock
Hickory, dickory, dock;
The mouse ran up the clock;
The clock struck one,
The mouse ran down,
Hickory, dickory, dock.

1. Which of these pairs is a rhyme?

   a. dock, one

   b. dock, clock

   c. one, down

2. Why did the mouse run?

   a. It could tell time.

   b. A cat chased it.

   c. The clock striking one scared it.

3. Look at the pair of items. Write one way in which they are alike and one way in which they are different.

   clocks and watches

   alike: _____

   different: _____

Name _____ Date _____

Analyzing a Poem

A poem
- *tells a writer's feelings about a topic.*
- *can tell how things are alike or different.*
- *can have rhyming words.*

Read the poem and the questions that follow. Underline the correct answer to each question.

The First Tooth

Through the house what busy joy,
Just because the infant boy
Has a tiny tooth to show!
I have got a double row,
All as white, and all as small;
Yet no one cares for mine at all.
He can say but half a word,

Yet that single sound's preferred
To all the words that I can say
In the longest summer day.
He cannot walk, yet if he put
With mimic motion out his foot,
As if he thought he were advancing,
It's prized more than my best dancing.
            ---Charles and Mary Lamb

1. Who is probably the speaker in this poem?

   a. baby boy

   b. the baby's older brother or sister

   c. the baby's father

2. What feelings does the speaker seem to have?

   a. The speaker is very happy with the baby.

   b. The speaker feels left out and jealous.

   c. The speaker does not even notice the baby.

3. Which of these pairs is a rhyme?

   a. joy, show   b. say, day   c. all, word

Name _____ Date _____

Evaluating to Compare and Contrast

To write a poem, good writers
- *study details.*
  - *tell how things are alike.*
    - *tell how things are different.*

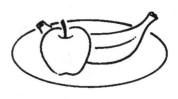

Look at each pair of items. Then write one way in which they are alike and one way in which they are different.

1. apples and bananas

   alike: _____

   different: _____

2. camels and horses

   alike: _____

   different: _____

3. flowers and perfume

   alike: _____

   different: _____

4. cars and buses

   alike: _____

   different: _____

Name _____ Date _____

Choosing Words to Paint a Vivid Picture

• Good writers choose words that paint a vivid picture.

Read each word picture. Underline the two things that are being compared. Then tell how they are alike.

1. The fog comes in like a cat.

   _____

2. The fog covered the top of the hill like a blanket.

   _____

3. The tree, like an umbrella, protected us from the rain.

   _____

4. The moon smiled down on us, just as Grandma always did.

   _____

5. The light reflected off the lake as if the lake were a mirror.

   _____

6. The grasshoppers called back and forth to each other like an echo in the mountains.

   _____

7. Like a knife through butter, the boat went through the water.

   _____

Unit 7: Poem
Writing Styles 3, SV 8056-1

Proofreading a Poem

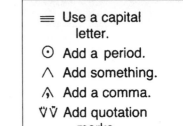

PROOFREADING HINT
To be a good proofreader, look for one type of error at a time.
For example, proofread once for capitalization errors, once
for punctuation errors, and once for spelling errors.

Proofread the poems, paying special attention to capital letters. Use the Proofreader's Marks to correct at least seven errors.

Peter Piper

peter Piper picked a peck of pickled peppers.

A peck of pickled peppers peter piper picked.

If peter Piper picked a peck of pickled peppers,

Where's the peck of pickled peppers Peter piper picked?

Mr. Nobody

i know a funny little man,

As quiet as a mouse,

Who does the mischief that is done

In everybody's house.

There's no won ever sees his face,

And yet we all agree

That every plate we brake was cracked

By mr. nobody.

Proofreader's Marks
≡ Use a capital letter.
⊙ Add a period.
∧ Add something.
⩘ Add a comma.
⌄⌄ Add quotation marks.
✂ Cut something.
⌃ Replace something.
∿ Transpose.
◯ Spell correctly.
¶ Indent paragraph.
/ Make a lowercase letter.

Write a Poem About a Tree

Look carefully at a tree you see every day. Do its leaves and colors remind you of other things? List some of the things you think of. Use your list to write a poem about the tree.

71

Name _____ Date _____

Write a Group Poem

Make a list of six items that you see every day. Write each word in a box. With a small group, cut out the boxes and mix them all up. Take turns choosing two words without looking at them first. Then write sentences that can be used to describe each item. Combine the sentences to make a group poem.

_____

_____

_____

_____

Write a Cloud Poem

Watch clouds as they change their shapes. List what things or animals their shapes remind you of. Write a poem about your clouds.

73

Name _____ Date _____

UNIT 8: Persuasive Paragraph
Assessment

Read the persuasive paragraph. Answer the questions that follow.

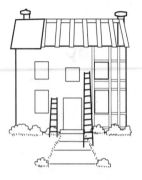

    The best building material for a house is bricks. A brick house always stays cool in summer and warm in winter. Houses made of wood need to be painted. Bricks never need to be painted. People get wet during the rainy season in a house made of straw. A brick house will keep people dry. Most importantly, a wolf cannot blow down a house made of bricks.

1. Draw a line under the topic sentence.

2. List the three main reasons the writer gives.

   _____

   _____

   _____

   _____

3. Which reason does the writer think is most important?

   _____

   _____

Name _____ Date _____

Analyzing a Persuasive Paragraph

> **A persuasive paragraph**
> - *tells the writer's feelings.*
> - *lists reasons.*
> - *asks readers to agree with the writer.*

Read the persuasive paragraph. Answer the questions that follow.

You should get involved in sports after school. There are many reasons for this. Perhaps the most important one is that exercise is good for your health. Exercise not only helps build strong muscles, it also helps keep your body from storing too much fat. A person who takes part in sports will usually have a healthier heart and lungs than a person who does not. In addition to being good for your health, sports can help you in other ways. Taking part in sports is a good way for you to make friends.

1. Draw a line under the topic sentence.

2. Does the topic sentence tell the writer's opinion?

   _____

3. What are the three main reasons the writer gives?

   _____

   _____

   _____

4. Which reason does the writer think is most important?

   _____

Unit 8: Persuasive Paragraph
Writing Styles 3, SV 8056-1

Name _____ Date _____

Evaluating to Draw Conclusions

✏️ • *To write a persuasive paragraph, good writers support their feelings with good reasons.*

Read each statement and the reasons that support it. Draw a line under the three best reasons.

1. Nathan pays for the bus to school, and he also buys his own lunch. Nathan thinks his allowance should be raised.
   a. His friend Orville gets more than he does.
   b. Lunch prices at school went up.
   c. He has been doing extra chores.
   d. Bus fares went up.
   e. He wants to start playing video games after school.

2. Dora's family is moving into a home that has two bedrooms for the three children. Dora thinks she should be the one to get her own room.
   a. She stays up later and doesn't want to disturb the others.
   b. She is the oldest and has more homework to do.
   c. She needs the extra space because she doesn't like to hang up her clothes.
   d. She needs the extra space for slumber parties.
   e. The other two children are boys, and it makes more sense for them to share a room.

Giving Reasons

> *Good writers*
> • *give good reasons to convince the reader.*

Read each sentence. Write the reason that best supports it. Choose from the reasons below.

1. You should do your homework before watching television.

   _____

2. You should save part of every allowance.

   _____

3. After you take your jacket off, hang it up.

   _____

4. You should try to be on time for appointments.

   _____

5. It is a good idea to be friendly to new students.

   _____

Reasons

It's not thoughtful to keep others waiting.

Clothes left lying around make the room messy.

You will have money for something big later.

Television takes time away from studies.

You might make a good friend this way.

Name _____ Date _____

Combining Sentences

- *Good writers sometimes combine sentences to make their writing more interesting.*
  - *Two short sentences might have the same subject. The writer writes the subject once and then combines the two predicates in the same sentence.*

Combine the predicates in these sentences. Write the new sentences.

1. Kathy was tired. Kathy wanted her lunch.

   _____

2. She turned smoothly in the water. She headed for the other end of the pool.

   _____

   _____

3. Kathy wanted to win. Kathy hoped to set records.

   _____

4. Kathy won many races. Kathy got many awards.

   _____

   _____

5. Kathy practiced as much as possible. Kathy competed with stronger swimmers.

   _____

   _____

Proofreading a Persuasive Paragraph

> ✋ PROOFREADING HINT
> *To be a good proofreader, look for one type of error at a time.*
> *For example, proofread once for capitalization errors, once*
> *for punctuation errors, and once for spelling errors.*

Proofread the persuasive paragraphs, paying special attention to words or letters that may be out of order. Use the Proofreader's Marks to correct at least seven errors.

Our class play coming is up next month, and everyone should hepl make it a success. It is true that not everyone can act in the play because there are not enough prats. Also, students some do not enjoy appearing on stage. Still, there is something for everyone do to. Those who do not wish to be on the stage can find plenty to do behind the scenes One such job making is scenery. Any student who likes to build can give time to this important job. We'll need staircases, walls, and street lamps for Act I. For Atc II we'll need scenery that looks like a beach

Proofreader's Marks
≡ Use a capital letter.
⊙ Add a period.
∧ Add something.
⩘ Add a comma.
ⱽⱽ Add quotation marks.
⚡ Cut something.
⋏ Replace something.
ⸯ Transpose.
◯ Spell correctly.
₦ Indent paragraph.
/ Make a lowercase letter.

Another important job is making costumes. Students who enjoy different kinds of clothes will have fun this with job. We'll need soem special hats, some jewelry, and some old-fashioned beach clothes.

Name _____ Date _____

Write About Pets

Talk with a partner about different kinds of pets. Together, choose a pet you would both like to have. Draw a picture of that pet. Write a paragraph telling why that animal would be a good pet.

Name _____ Date _____

Write About Your Home

With another student, make a list of things you like about your town. Then write three sentences that tell why your town is a great place to live.

Things I like about my town

_____   _____

_____   _____

_____   _____

_____   _____

Why Our Town Is a Great Place to Live

_____

_____

_____

_____

_____

_____

Name _____ Date _____

Write Your Opinion

With a small group, consider this question: Should third-graders learn to do their own laundry? At the top of this sheet write your answer and one reason that supports it. Everyone in the group shares answers. Then, using your reason and others from your group, write a persuasive paragraph to answer the question.

Should third-graders learn to do their own laundry?

_____ yes   _____ no

Name _____ Date _____

Write About a Movie

With several other students, plan and write five sentences about a movie you all like. Revise and proofread your sentences.

_____

_____

_____

_____

_____

_____

Draw a movie poster for your film.

Unit 8: Persuasive Paragraph
Writing Styles 3, SV 8056-1

Name _____ Date _____

Write About Actions People Can Take

Here are statements about actions people can take. Check the statement that you feel the most strongly about and for which you have good reasons. Write a paragraph to convince someone to agree with you.

☐ Everyone should learn to cook.

☐ Everyone should go camping.

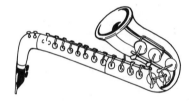

☐ Everyone should play a musical instrument.

_____

_____

_____

_____

_____

_____

Name _____ Date _____

UNIT 9: Research Report
Assessment

**Read this research report. Underline the
correct answer to each question.**

Thomas Edison, Great Inventor

We see Thomas Edison's inventions
everywhere. You often use his inventions.
Without him, you could never turn on a light.
Films are shown through one of his inventions.
Music is listened to on one of his inventions.

Edison invented the electric lamp in 1879. He invented
the movie projector and the phonograph. Edison is the greatest
inventor who ever lived. He invented over 1,000 things!

1. The topic of this report is
   a. what Thomas Edison invented.
   b. how Thomas Edison invented the electric lamp.
   c. how a movie projector works.

2. What is one detail about the main idea?
   a. Thomas Edison lived in the 1800s.
   b. Edison invented the phonograph.
   c. You can not turn on a light.

3. Which sentence states an opinion?
   a. Edison is the greatest inventor who ever lived.
   b. Edison invented the electric lamp in 1879.
   c. Films are shown through one of his inventions.

Name _____ Date _____

Analyzing a Research Report

A research report
- *gives facts about one topic.*
- *usually has more than one paragraph.*
- *has a title that tells about the topic.*

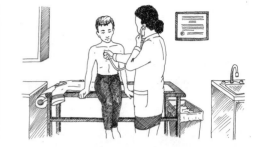

Read this part of a research report. Answer the questions.

A cold is caused by a virus. No one really knows how to prevent colds. Getting wet or chilled does not directly give you a cold. A chill, however, might put you in a weaker state than usual. Then, if a cold is going around, you will be more likely to get it.

Colds are usually caught by being near someone who already has one. The easiest way to catch a cold is from someone's sneeze. One person with a cold in a crowd can give it to many other people just by sneezing. If you have a cold, you should stay away from other people.

1. What is the topic of this report?

   _____

2. Write the sentence that states the main idea.

   _____

3. What is one detail about the main idea?

   _____

   _____

4. What might the topic of another paragraph in this research paper be?

   _____

Name _____ Date _____

Classifying Fact and Opinion

> ✏️ *To write a research report, good writers*
> • *include only facts about the topic.*

Read each sentence. Write *fact* or *opinion* to tell what it is.

_____ 1. Liquid is a necessary ingredient of soup.

_____ 2. Chicken soup is better than turkey soup.

_____ 3. Gabriel's Restaurant serves lamb stew.

_____ 4. Gabriel's Restaurant serves good lamb stew.

_____ 5. The dishwasher is broken.

_____ 6. Every home should have a dishwasher.

_____ 7. We eat fish every Sunday.

_____ 8. Fish can be prepared in many ways.

_____ 9. Tuna is the most delicious fish you can buy.

_____ 10. The Japanese people eat a lot of fish.

_____ 11. Gabriel's Restaurant has one high chair.

_____ 12. People should not bring babies to restaurants.

Name _____ Date _____

Using Exact Words

> ✏️ *Good writers*
> • *use exact words to tell the facts about a topic.*

Read each sentence. From the word list, choose a more exact word or phrase to replace each underlined word or phrase. Write a new sentence with the more exact words.

Word List
1. cat, dog, hamster -- bedroom, living room, kitchen
2. sleeping, napping, dozing -- an hour, about two hours
3. liver, hamburger, spinach - chopped, grilled, steamed
4. run, walk, exercise
5. ball, stuffed mouse, exercise wheel

1. My <u>pet</u> sat on the sill of the window in the <u>room</u>.

_____

2. He was <u>resting</u> for <u>a little while</u>.

_____

3. Soon it would be time to eat some <u>food</u>, which I had <u>fixed</u> for him.

_____

4. In the afternoon, my pet would want to <u>play</u>.

_____

5. I need to buy a new <u>toy</u> for my pet.

_____

Expanding Sentences

> ✏ • *Good writers make sentences clear by using adjectives and adverbs that describe the topic exactly.*

Add an adjective or an adverb where you see this mark: *. The word or words you add should describe the thing or action. Write your new sentences.

1. The * hummingbird built a * nest.

   _____

   _____

2. She found a * tree in a * place.

   _____

   _____

3. She wanted her nest to be * away from * cats.

   _____

   _____

4. She laid * eggs and sat on them *.

   _____

   _____

5. * the eggs hatched and the babies cried * for food.

   _____

   _____

Proofreading a Research Project

> ✋ PROOFREADING HINT
> *To be a good proofreader, look for one type of error at a time.*
> *For example, proofread once for capitalization errors, once*
> *for punctuation errors, and once for spelling errors.*

Proofread the beginning of a research report, paying special attention to spelling. Use the Proofreader's Marks to correct at least six errors.

The Passenger Pigeon

At one time there was a kind of bird called the passenger pigeon. The passenger pigeon was one of the most common birds in the wirld. In fact, their were once so many passenger pigeons that they darkened the skies. One sumar day these birds completely blocked the sunshine in New york. In 1808 poepel saw a flock of passenger pigeons one mile wide and 240 miles long! the flock had over two billyon birds. The birds in that flock ate about 434,000 bushels of nuts, rice, and berrys every day.

No one now can see even won living passenger pigeon The last wild passenger pigeon was killed in 1906 in connecticut. In 1914 the last passenger pigeon in a zoo died. the passenger pigeon is extinct.

Proofreader's Marks	
≡	Use a capital letter.
⊙	Add a period.
∧	Add something.
⋀	Add a comma.
ⱽⱽ	Add quotation marks.
✂	Cut something.
⋀	Replace something.
⏦	Transpose.
◯	Spell correctly.
⊓	Indent paragraph.
/	Make a lowercase letter.

Name _____ Date _____

Write About Animal Nests

Many different kinds of animals build nests. With several other students, read about one kind of nest. Draw a picture of this nest. Together with the students, write at least four sentences about the animal and its nest.

_____

_____

_____

_____

_____

_____

Name _____ Date _____

Make a Bird Book

Work with several other students. Together, read about one unusual kind of bird. Draw pictures to show what the bird looks like, where it lives, what it eats, and what is special about it. Write two sentences to go with each picture.

What It Looks Like

Where It Lives

What It Eats

What Is Special About It

Write About Robots

With several other students, read about robots. Find out what kinds of jobs robots can do. Draw a picture of one type of robot, and write at least five sentences telling what that robot can do.

_____

_____

_____

_____

_____

_____

Unit 9: Research Report
Writing Styles 3, SV 8056-1

Name _____ Date _____

Write About Birds

With a partner, choose one kind of sea bird to write about. Together, find five facts about this bird. Then write five sentences about it.

Sea Bird Facts

_____   _____

_____   _____

_____

_____

_____

_____

_____

_____

_____

_____

WRITING STYLES: GRADE 3
ANSWER KEY

Unit 1: Personal Narrative
Assessment, p. 9
1. middle 2. beginning 3. ending
4. Responses will vary. Be sure reason given is valid.
P. 10
1. ending 2. beginning 3. middle
4. ending 5. middle 6. beginning
P. 11
1. 2, 3, 1 2. 1, 3, 2
P. 12
Responses will vary. Be sure reasons given are valid.
P. 13
1. receive 2. fortunate 3. bad
4. require 5. buy 6. least 7. cruel
P. 14

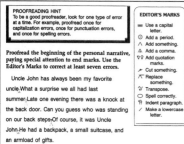

Unit 2: Information Paragraph
Assessment, p. 18
Main idea: Animal tracks can tell you many things. 1., 2. Sentences will vary. Be sure that details refer to the main idea. 3. Paragraph B is more interesting because there are more details and examples. 4. Responses will vary, but should correctly give a detail from the paragraph.
P. 19
1. Main idea: The squid and the octopus look very different. a., b. Sentences will vary. Be sure that details refer to the main idea. 2. The squid and the octopus behave very differently. a., b. Sentences will vary. Be sure that details refer to the main idea.
P. 20
1. a. detail b. detail c. main idea
d. detail 2. a. detail b. detail c. detail
d. main idea
P. 21
Possible responses:
1. The second paragraph is more interesting because there are more details and examples. 2. Responses will vary, but should correctly give a detail from the paragraph. 3. Responses will vary, but should correctly give a detail from the paragraph.
P. 22
A sighted person can only imagine what it is like to be blind. Put a scarf over your eyes to block out light. Try to figure out what different foods are. Pretend to pay for something with

coins. Try to walk into another room and sit at a table. Blind people can do all these things and more.
P. 23

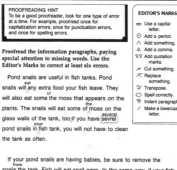

Unit 3: Friendly Letter
Assessment, p. 27
1. b 2. a. 3. Rosa wants to thank her aunt for the shirt. 4. October 8, 1998. We know because of the date. 5. Rosa wrote the letter. We know because of the signature.
P. 28
1. 486 Amigo Avenue
    San Diego, California 92116
    April 14, 1999
2. Dear Roberto, 3. Your friend,
4. Your cousin, 5. Dear Alice, 6. b 7. c
8. c
P. 29
1. a. detail b. detail c. summary
d. detail e. detail 2. a. detail b. detail
c. detail d. summary e. detail
P. 30
1. Mimi wants to thank her grandparents and to tell them about her report. 2. Mimi's grandparents are the audience. We know because of the greeting. 3. Mimi wrote the letter. We know because of the signature.
P. 31
1. Inventions make our lives easier, and we take them for granted. 2. We get cold, and we turn on a heater. 3. Long ago people got cold, and they sat around a fire. 4. A very long time ago, people had no fire, and they stayed cold.
5. Our heater works, and we stay warm.
P. 32

Unit 4: How-to Paragraph
Assessment, p. 36
1. how to make a tie-dyed shirt 2. start, next, then, finally 3. Remove all the rubber bands.
P. 37
Possible responses: 1. how to fry an egg 2. an egg, a tablespoon of butter, a frying pan with a cover, a teaspoon of water, and a spatula 3. first, after that, then, finally 4. second, then, the second thing you do is
P. 38
A.1. Put toothpaste on your brush.
2. Check books out at librarian's desk.
B. 3, 2, 4, 1
P. 39
1. Get four popsicle sticks and some white glue. 2. Get six light-colored beans and six dark-colored ones.
3. the first thing, then, next, after that, the last thing 4. second, next, the second thing you do is
P. 40
1. Pet mice can be black, red, or silver.
2. Other colors for mice include gray, cream, and white. 3. A mouse can chew on wood, nuts, and twigs. 4. Mice clean their own bodies, faces, and ears.
5. Soup cans are good resting places for pet mice, hamsters, and gerbils.
P. 41

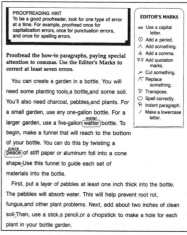

Unit 5: Descriptive Paragraph
Assessment, p. 46
1. a. 2. c 3. Casey has a tail. Casey said, "Meow."
P. 47
1. thick, red 2. round 3. green, orange
4. two-story, tiny 5. huge 6. little, brown 7. colorful 8. loud, banging
9. terrific 10. delicious 11. spicy, tender
P. 48
1. b 2. c 3. a 4. b
P. 49
1. look 2. feel 3. sound 4. look
5. sound 6. look 7. look 8. taste 9. feel
10. smell
P. 50
1. Guppies and goldfish are pets for fish tanks. 2. Catfish and snails clean harmful moss from the tank. 3. Black mollies and goldfish are lovely fish.
4. Guppies and black mollies have live

babies. 5. Zebra fish and angelfish lay eggs.

P. 51

PROOFREADING HINT
To be a good proofreader, look for one type of error at a time. For example, proofread once for capitalization errors, once for punctuation errors, and once for spelling errors.

EDITOR'S MARKS
≡ Use a capital letter.
⊙ Add a period.
∧ Add something.
⋏ Add a comma.
∀∇ Add quotation marks.
✄ Cut something.
⌒ Replace something.
∩ Transpose.
○ Spell correctly.
¶ Indent paragraph.
/ Make a lowercase letter.

Proofread the descriptive paragraphs, paying special attention to the verbs that go with sentence subjects. Use the Editor's Marks to correct at least seven errors.

Have you ever heard of a person who likes washing dishes? My friend Dan really enjoy it. In fact, Dan washes dishes whenever he can. Dan pull a chair over to the sink so he can reach everything easily. Dan likes the lemony smell of the liquid detergent. He squeezes the bottle gently and watches the liquid soap stream into the water. The soap mix with the hot water. Together, they create a mass of frothy white bubbles. When the bubbles almost reach the top of the sink, Dan turns the water off. then he carefully puts the glasses into the water.

Most of all, Dan like using a brand-new dishcloth. The cloth feel soft in Dan's hands. It has a clean smell, too. Dan rub each glass carefully with the soft, new cloth. Then he rinses the glass and sets it on the drainer.

Unit 6: Story
Assessment, p. 57
Possible responses:
1. school 2. Mr. McGrath finds the pets too noisy. 3. a 4. b

P. 58
Possible responses:
1. King Midas 2. Greece long ago
3. The golden touch has made his food, drink, and daughter turn to gold.
4. Even his food and drink turned to gold. 5. King Midas had to beg to have his golden touch taken away.

P. 59
1. Girl sits by stream. 2. Rabbit runs by. 3. Rabbit goes down a hole.
4. Rabbit has vest on. 5. Rabbit has a watch. 6. Rabbit talks. 7. real 8. real
9. make-believe 10. make-believe

P. 60
1. a 2. b 3. c 4. c

P. 61
1. The baby opened the cabinet. She took out all the pots. 2. The mother came into the kitchen. She saw the mess. 3. The mother smiled at the baby. She asked if it was fun. 4. The baby smiled back. She was having a good time. 5. The mother sat on the floor. She played with the baby.

P. 62

PROOFREADING HINT
To be a good proofreader, look for one type of error at a time. For example, proofread once for capitalization errors, once for punctuation errors, and once for spelling errors.

EDITOR'S MARKS
≡ Use a capital letter.
⊙ Add a period.
∧ Add something.
⋏ Add a comma.
∀∇ Add quotation marks.
✄ Cut something.
⌒ Replace something.
∩ Transpose.
○ Spell correctly.
¶ Indent paragraph.
/ Make a lowercase letter.

Proofread the stories, paying special attention to capital letters at the beginning of sentences. Use the Editor's Marks to correct at least six errors.

1. Fox looked up at the grapes on the vine. how delicious they seemed! he decided to have some grapes four his lunch. The grapes were quite high, and it was hard for Fox to reach them. he stretched and jumped, but he couldn't get the grapes. Fox tried again and again. the grapes always seemed just out of reach. Finally, Fox gave up. he walked away, asking himself, "Who would want those sour old grapes?"

2. Goldilocks sat down at the bears' table. the first chair she tried was too hard, and the second chair was too soft. the third chair felt just right. Next, Goldilocks tried all the oatmeal on the table. The first bowl was too hot, and the second bowl was too cold. The third bowl tasted just right. after she had eaten the whole bowl of oatmeal, Goldilocks went upstairs for a nap.

Unit 7: Poem
Assessment, p. 66
1. b 2. c 3. Accept reasonable responses.

P. 67
1. b 2. b 3. b

P. 68
Possible responses:
1. alike: Both are fruits. Both can be eaten raw. different: Their shapes are different. Bananas grow in bunches, and apples do not. 2. alike: Both are mammals. Both can carry things on their backs. different: Camels have humps, and horses do not. Camels like deserts; horses do not. 3. alike: Both smell good. Both can lose their good smell. different: Flowers are living; perfume is not. Perfume is a liquid; flowers are not. 4. alike: Both are ways to travel. Both have wheels. different: Cars are smaller. Buses can hold many passengers.

P. 69
1. fog, cat — Both are quiet, and you can't hear them coming. 2. fog, blanket — Both cover something so you can't see what's underneath. 3. tree, umbrella — Both provide shelter.
4. moon, Grandma — Both make the speaker feel good by seeming to smile.
5. lake, mirror — Both the lake and the mirror reflect light. 6. grasshoppers, echo — Both seem to respond right away. 7. knife, boat —Both move quietly and easily.

P. 70

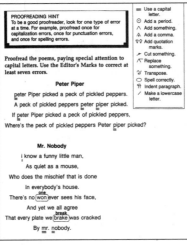

PROOFREADING HINT
To be a good proofreader, look for one type of error at a time. For example, proofread once for capitalization errors, once for punctuation errors, and once for spelling errors.

EDITOR'S MARKS
≡ Use a capital letter.
⊙ Add a period.
∧ Add something.
⋏ Add a comma.
∀∇ Add quotation marks.
✄ Cut something.
⌒ Replace something.
∩ Transpose.
○ Spell correctly.
¶ Indent paragraph.
/ Make a lowercase letter.

Proofread the poems, paying special attention to capital letters. Use the Editor's Marks to correct at least seven errors.

Peter Piper
peter Piper picked a peck of pickled peppers.
A peck of pickled peppers peter piper picked.
If peter Piper picked a peck of pickled peppers,
Where's the peck of pickled peppers Peter piper picked?

Mr. Nobody
i know a funny little man,
As quiet as a mouse,
Who does the mischief that is done
In everybody's house.
There's no one won ever sees his face,
And yet we all agree
That every plate we break brake was cracked
By mr. nobody.

Unit 8: Persuasive Paragraph
Assessment, p. 74
1. The best building material for a house is bricks. 2. Possible responses: A brick house stays cool in summer and warm in winter. A brick house will keep people dry. A wolf can not blow down a house made of bricks. 3. That a wolf can not blow down a house made of bricks.

P. 75
1. You should get involved in sports after school. 2. yes 3. Possible responses: Exercise is important for good physical health. Exercise builds strong muscles; exercise keeps the body from storing fat; and exercise builds healthy heart and lungs. 4. It is important for your health.

P. 76
1. b, c, d 2. a, b, e

P. 77
1. Television takes time away from studies. 2. You will have money for something big later. 3. Clothes left lying around make the room messy.
4. It's not thoughtful to keep others waiting. 5. You might make a good friend this way.

P. 78
1. Kathy was tired and wanted her lunch. 2. She turned smoothly in the water and headed for the other end of the pool. 3. Kathy wanted to win and hoped to set records. 4. Kathy won many races and got many awards.
5. Kathy practiced as much as possible and competed with stronger swimmers.

P. 79

PROOFREADING HINT
To be a good proofreader, look for one type of error at a time. For example, proofread once for capitalization errors, once for punctuation errors, and once for spelling errors.

EDITOR'S MARKS
≡ Use a capital letter.
⊙ Add a period.
∧ Add something.
⋏ Add a comma.
∀∇ Add quotation marks.
✄ Cut something.
⌒ Replace something.
∩ Transpose.
○ Spell correctly.
¶ Indent paragraph.
/ Make a lowercase letter.

Proofread the persuasive paragraphs, paying special attention to words or letters that may be out of order. Use the Editor's Marks to correct at least seven errors.

Our class play coming is up next month, and everyone should help make it a success. It is true that not everyone can act in the play because there are not are enough prats. Also, students some do not enjoy appearing on stage. Still, there is something for everyone do to. Those who do not wish to be on the stage can find plenty to do behind the scenes. One such job making is scenery. Any student who likes to build can give time to this important job. We'll need staircases, walls, and street lamps for Act I. For Act II we'll need scenery that looks like a beach.

Another important job is making costumes. Students who enjoy different kinds of clothes will have fun this with job. We'll need some special hats, some jewelry, and some old-fashioned beach clothes.

Unit 9: Research Report
Assessment, p. 85
1. a 2. b 3. a

P. 86
1. colds 2. A cold is caused by a virus.
3. Responses will vary. 4. Responses will vary.

P. 87
1. fact 2. opinion 3. fact 4. opinion
5. fact 6. opinion 7. fact 8. fact
9. opinion 10. fact 11. fact 12. opinion

P. 88
Responses will vary.

P. 89
Accept any reasonable responses.

P. 90

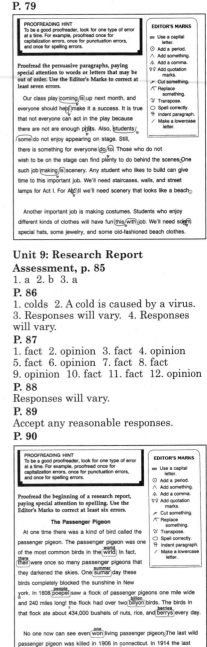

PROOFREADING HINT
To be a good proofreader, look for one type of error at a time. For example, proofread once for capitalization errors, once for punctuation errors, and once for spelling errors.

EDITOR'S MARKS
≡ Use a capital letter.
⊙ Add a period.
∧ Add something.
⋏ Add a comma.
∀∇ Add quotation marks.
✄ Cut something.
⌒ Replace something.
∩ Transpose.
○ Spell correctly.
¶ Indent paragraph.
/ Make a lowercase letter.

Proofread the beginning of a research report, paying special attention to spelling. Use the Editor's Marks to correct at least six errors.

The Passenger Pigeon
At one time there was a kind of bird called the passenger pigeon. The passenger pigeon was one of the most common birds in the wirld world. In fact, their there were once so many passenger pigeons that they darkened the skies. One sumar summer day these birds completely blocked the sunshine in New york. In 1808 poepel people saw a flock of passenger pigeons one mile wide and 240 miles long! The flock had over two billyon billion birds. The birds in that flock ate about 434,000 bushels of nuts, rice, and berrys berries every day.

No one now can see even won one living passenger pigeon. The last wild passenger pigeon was killed in 1906 in connecticut. In 1914 the last passenger pigeon in a zoo died. the passenger pigeon is extinct.